Publication Details

Title: *Alive Is What You Feel*
ISBN: 978-1-925963-63-2 (hbk)
ISBN: 978-1-925963-62-5 (pbk)
ISBN 978-1-925963-64-9 (e-bk)

Published by Wild Arancini Press
Copyright © 2023 Frank Prem
All Images Copyright © 2023 Frank Prem

Originally published by Wild Arancini Press:

Walk Away, Silver Heart 2020
ISBN: 978-1-925963-06-9 p-bk
ISBN: 978-1-925963-01-4 e-bk

A Kiss for the Worthy 2020
ISBN: 978-1-925963-04-5 p-bk
ISBN: 978-1-925963-05-2 e-bk

Rescue and Redemption 2020
ISBN: 978-0-9751442-9-9 p-bk
ISBN: 978-1-925963-03-8 e-bk

ALIVE

is what you feel

A Love Poetry Trilogy
Omnibus Edition

FRANK PREM

Contents

*Let this homage be to their honour and this lesser path
lead you home.*

About: The Love Poetry Trilogy

The Love Poetry Trilogy is comprised of three poetry collections, each inspired by a particular piece of poetry written by stellar poets, over a century ago.

The origin of this work goes back a number of years to an occasion when I was fortunate to participate in a project that involved individual poets located around the globe.

Each poet chose a phrase from the body of a distinguished poem written long in the past, and used that phrase as inspiration for a piece of new poetry. New and old were then hyperlinked together to create an interactive work.

Over the course of the project, three poems (and their poets) were chosen as source material for the experiment:

Amy Lowell – *Madonna of the Evening Flowers* (1919)
Walt Whitman – *Leaves of Grass* (1855) Parts 1 and 2
T.S. Eliot - *The Love Song of J Alfred Prufrock* (1915) (Epigraph, plus Stanzas 1 – 5)

To the best of my knowledge, no trace remains of the original project, but I was recently inspired to revisit and to continue an exploration of the effects these wonderful poems might have on my own work.

Each source poem commanded its own identifiable voice in my responses, and is discussed further in a later section of this book. I will say here only that in each case, I found the source poems to be concerned with love, in one form or another, and thus *The Love Poetry Trilogy*.

FP
2023

Walk Away Silver Heart Part 1

For the poets who have gone before me. May they ever continue to inspire.

For my loved ones, all.

a small piece (free)

All day long I have been working

all the day
I
am working

toil
required to keep fuel
on the fire

and the table
well laden

I do
what I must
to ensure
all is
what it should be

yet
through each of those hours
I dream

inhabit
desire

and a yearning

to be home
to be with you

to be one
with my own spaces and places
well known

defined

all the day long
I have been
working as I know I must do
but
all the day long
too
I have nurtured
my heart

kept a piece
one small piece of it
free
and untrammelled
by need

or other
mundane requirement

I have placed it
in my mind
right there
beside you

our backs
warmed together
by fire

well nourished (now to sleep)

Now I am tired

I have gazed
up
at the sky
all morning

placed my nose
right in close
to smell
the sweet perfume
that comes
from blossom

in the garden
I have studied
the ways that green grass
grows

noting
that it did not move
at all
like this
in the winter

and listening
to birds
has taken more time
than anticipated

until
I find the day has fled
on wings
while I pursued it
on foot

I am tired now
with
nothing done

I am wearied
from my thoughts
and observations

I do believe
I need to rest
or
my senses may
explode

but this day

this wondrous day
has brought nourishment
for my soul

from a confusion (of insensible things)

I call: "Where are you?"

in the night

awakened
from a deep dream
that is a confusion
playing its dishevelment
as though a conversation
of insensible things
shared
between rational beings

my eyes open
staring at the darkness

startled

I call
where are you
but the silence is a hollow
swallowing sound and equilibrium
in a single gloating

I find that I am panting
and the feeling
of the heart
within my chest
is the gallop
of a panicked steed

I must rise
find the light switch

I need to feel the floor
unmoving
beneath my feet
as I stagger to the kitchen sink
to find a glass of water

to find a calming
that might last me through
until dawn

sough leaves and heartbeat moments (stolen)

But there is only the oak tree rustling in the wind

I
listen in the night
when you are gone
away

keep imagining
the car wheels
turning

the sound of gravel
crushed
beneath tyres

and I think that I can hear
the purring
of the engine

coming home

but no
you have hardly gone

the long hours
stretch
before me

and the sound
I can hear
is only the oak tree
rustling

as the wind
ruffles through
the sough leaves

I turn away

toss and roll

the bed
beneath me
has hardened

there is no comfort
to be had
from lying still
and wondering

about you
and the road

about the place
you are
and where you've been

the night to come
and the long hours
still
before me

the oak tree
sighs

the wind
is her accomplice

and every breath
she sounds
is another moment
taken

I will lose one more
the same
with every heartbeat
(at least)
until you get home

been away (bearing home)

The house is very quiet

been away

now
here I am

I cast my eyes
into the silence

nothing to see

the house
is very quiet

the hum
of a refrigerator
the only song

I walk
from room to room
to inspect the stillness

the hush

only
an arrangement
of teddy bears
is present

you have left them
to greet me

an interim
to hold

to tide me
over

I look around

the space is large

but the house
seems small

diminished
in spirit

every time
I journey
it is the same

only the soft fur
of the leading bear
can make
these first
empty moments
feel
like home

morning (awaited)

The sun shines in on your books

there is
a lazy ray
of sunshine

lying across the pages
of a philosophy

a
how to live
guide

pick it up
I
place it back down

it has become
a tedious thing

a randomness
of ideas
with you not here
to share it

and the stealthy sun
has crept away
its beam of light
dimmed
to dull
by increasing distance

the only philosophy
I can hold
right now
is getting through
each day

and wondering
what I should do
to fill the surplus minutes
every hour

until
with one last
gleam of fading sun

the night

becomes

and I
await
the morning

the way you wield (flashes in the light)

On your scissors and thimble just put down

I watch
the way you wield
your scissors

they flash in the light

attract my eye

and I see the threads
one by one
trimmed even

the needle darts
in its rhythmic
pattern

as the sewing machine
whirs

the replacement
of a button

a running repair
to my *outside* pants

become works
of an artisan craft
that I try to capture
together with your scissors
and your reels of cotton
on paper

with a pencil

but . . .

you are done
your tools
stowed

scissors in a box

needle
in its cushion

sewing machine
wheeled away
to a private corner

while I
run hands
through hair
contemplating a way
to stitch together
an opening line
to describe
this meditation

that catches my eye
as it flashes
in the light

needle
and cotton
and scissors

too much (to bear)

But you are not there

the chill
that touches
around my shoulders
is
a clue

the weight
within the silence
is another

I make a noise
while opening the door
but the quiet
dominates my sounds

I look around
momentarily
to find you

the hallway seems
a chasm
filled up
with emptiness
distilled

I look around
again
to find you

you're not there

you are
somewhere away

in sydney
this time

somewhere
beyond the great divide

when you said
you would be gone
for a few days
it didn't seem like
such an age

but you
are in sydney
and
this silence
is

too many minutes

too many hours

too many
days
and
just too much

you are coming
home
on the evening flight

the house
is waiting

and the soft plush bears
are waiting

the silence
is waiting

and for this
soft bear
it is
just
too much

suddenly (the sun)

Suddenly I am lonely

suddenly
the cloud
appears

suddenly
the sun is gone

look around
I look around
at nothing

suddenly
the sound
is a bark

suddenly
dogs howling

listen
I listen hard
to sounds
akin to anger

and the day
has changed

the spark
is gone

what was sunshine
and gold
all at once
is grey

suddenly
I find . . .

myself

suddenly
I am all
that is here

and suddenly in emptiness
I am lonely
and I wonder
what has changed

where
are you now

did you take my day
the sun
away
with you

suddenly

so
suddenly

here

Where are you?

I turn
to see you

you are not
there
anymore

I turn round
and
around again

seeking your shape
in the shadows

in footprints
across the floor

through the glass
slightly speckled
of the kitchen window
that leads my eye
outside

out
to the garden
where a shape
that is perhaps
just a shift of the sun
suggests
something of you

but
no
I don't think so

and I wonder
where have you gone

where are you
at this moment
when
I am seeking you
with a stray thought

an idea
that came into my mind

I
have a need
to share
to speak
to hear your reply
to this whim of mine

and I am
forlorn
for
I did not see you
depart

another sign
of my chronic
inattentiveness

I know

I know

I tell myself
berating

I must pay you
more mind

must notice where
you are going
what
you are doing

why it is
that you flit
from my mind
when I . . .

I preoccupy
the whole of me
with trivia

just trivia
that I believe might be
interesting

engaging to you

yet
I know
that is not so

it is not
really
so

and
all that is left
is to wait for you

quietly . . .

attentively . . .

thoughtfully . . .

distractedly . . .

absorbedly . . .

preoccupied-ly . . .

.

.

.

I am gone
inside myself
and my thoughts
again

you have returned
and I
did not notice
but suddenly you
are here

listening
to my story
which is now gushing out
not at all rational

you are here
and you listen

and
I think
that you know
everything
that there is
to know

about me

waiting

I go about searching

the day begins

alone

I wander
around the house

perform
perfunctory tasks

clean away
the dishes

rake the grate
and set
the fire

but
do not light it

this becomes a search
for
new purposes

.

.

.

today

today

it has only been
an hour
or two

it will only be
a day

but
so long
is a moment
stretched in time

so very long
is the passage
of a cloud that moves
relentlessly
across the sky

from west
to east

I would turn
the day back
to not so long ago

east
to west
or push it
forward
to the next time

I search
myself
this time
for meaning

and
finding none
wander empty

through room
after room

into day

Then I see you

and today
the clouds
come low

grey
surrounds my head
covers
my eyes

I walk
in blindness

stumbling forward

touch
replaces sight

what I feel
is all I see

and all I touch
is cloud
is grey
to my senses

I
walking blind

in the heart
of nothing

then
you
are revealed

sun
is stronger
than cloud

it is you
in the light

the night
becomes day
and . . .

I see you

I think (I paint)

I think
of summer

leaves open
like
a fluttering of flags
to adorn
deciduous trees

I think
a pastel t-shirt

and think the wide brim
of a straw sunhat
too

barefoot
lightly upon a path

a twirl
with a basket full
of picked greens
and vegetables

I watch my thought
skip
and dance

watch
those leaves

I paint the straw hat

establish
the t-shirt

dab the zucchini

you . . .

paint your green leaves
too

finding me (a warm place carried)

Standing under a spire of pale blue larkspur

I
beneath the pandorea

even
standing at my tallest
it towers above me

a floral wall
of hanging bells
in
creamy white

you are one
with the secateurs
cutting where you will

your ornaments

adornments
and pretties
for arrangement

a vase

you seem
to stop
your arm stilled
eyes fixed
on me

I am something . . .

something . . .

not expected

I wait on you

your leisure

the time needed
for a surprise
to pass
and you to raise me

like a talisman
a love mote
from the garden

a warm place
to be carried
close
to where *you* are

where you *live*

the being
of you

made more

more
than one pandorea
of cream
and white

murmuring (the lake)

You are cool, like silver

the water stills
as though
it has never
been disturbed

strange

I watch the place
where you submerged

see reflections

it is evening
and the moon
is rising hugely
on the horizon

the water shimmers
a trail of light
murmuring
even in the stillness

and you arise
cool to touch
right before my eyes

a personification
of the silver night

and laughing
while the water
streams

in rivulets
of moonshine

behind you
the water shimmers
to its own
murmurings

need (goes on)

I become
a thing
of need

a hunger in the night time
ravening

desiring

and wanting

a rampage
when I'm standing still

emotions
all the time
racing

running

leaping
while I fear
I'll fall

fear
that I have fallen
already

deep
delves each feeling
each pounding
pummelling
of uncontrolled
sensation

and I don't know
what I
should do

don't know
how
to create calm space
that I might fall
in
to

and you smile
at me

have me wondering
did I see
what I saw

did it mean
what I thought

was it intended
for me

do you smile
like that
at everyone

at anyone

at someone else . . .

I become a thing
that is fully lost

I become a doubt

no trust
or faith
just gnawing

and still
I need . . .

something

still I want . . .

something

still
I long

still I hope

still
I wish . . .

for something

and go on
bleeding

chiming a little tune (of you)

I think the Canterbury bells are playing little tunes

I think
that I heard the bells
as you
brushed past

playing little
tinkling
riffs

when they touched

one
into
the next one
rang

and one
again

into another

    ting
    tong
    tang

as I listened
I believe I heard
a small tune
of you

yes

I believe
I heard them sing
your name

ting

ting-a-ling

tang
tong
tang

and ting

ting

tang-a-lang tong

they sang your name

at least
that
is what I heard

the breeze
when I closed my eyes
was like
your fingers
wandering
through my hair

and as it ruffled me
I heard the bells . . .

ting tang
tang
tong

. . . call aloud
your name

for the summer

You tell me that the peonies need spraying

and now
with the spring season
upon us
and the summer
set
to bloom hot and dry
and long
you point me
towards the new garden bed

especially
the pineapple sage
that bloomed
so prolifically
in its first year

its need for care

if the whole of the bed
is to grow
as we have planned
room must be made

for the pittosporum
to hedge
and the waratahs
to transform
from seedling
to tree

through every season
we must tend
these things
that we so
love

snipping

touching

and inhaling

there is joy
in this

joy that comes
from your hand
and mine
tilling with our fingers

moulding
with implements

at the approach
of summer

bounds overrun (by aquilegias)

That the columbines have overrun all bounds

the aquilegias
have restless hearts

they have burst
beyond their bounds

we should have known
they would be
beyond containing

pretty flowers
they respond
to love

and water
and fertilizer

are they not
like you
and me

and
do we not
bloom
beneath the warming sun

a fair
display

of
you and I

red and pink the blossom

That the pyrus japonica should be cut back and rounded

I broke
a branch
off the japonica

I have always thought
the red
quite beautiful

I find
specimens
in odd corners
of strange gardens
that I pass by
on the street

not cut back
or rounded
but growing wild

a little
unkempt

I grasp a branch
work it
to and fro
to break free

the red blossoms
in my hand
are a picture

and
in another place
another
ignored backyard tangle
there is a neglected peach

a prettiness
of petals
and stamens

I bring them home
and hope
that you will know
what I was thinking

when I chose
each branch of blossom
for you

tell me everything (about you)

talk to me

tell me things
you think
I need
to know

pour your ideas
red
into my wine glass

speak of love

talk in tongues
of fire

tell me of your anger

of the passion
that is the same thing

shout aloud
all the things
that *you* believe
hold meaning

I will turn them
with a flourish
of phrasing
into a word song

ta-da ta-da-da

throw your glass
into the fire

then
start dancing

tell me
all these things

I
would know
everything
and all there is

about you

walk away (silver heart)

But I look at you, heart of silver

silver heart
I look at you

see myself
as
I should have been

but something pure
was lost
along the way

I don't glance
backward
do not check my stride
but

I look at you
heart of silver
and wonder why you
look at me

I believe
you see my
might have
and my *could*

if some small part
of you
were surrendered
to become a part
of me

you choose
not to see
what I have been
and done

but only catch
the darkness
in my eyes

and fall
into a dream
of me

silver heart
I look at you . . .
and wonder

will you walk
away

and again

White heart-flame of polished silver

I hear
the song

I have heard it now
almost
forever

your lustred hair
has changed a shade
or two
from
copper shine
to this smooth
and polished
silver

but not the song

your voice
is young
still
and again

I hear it
as a young man hears

for that
is how it comes
to me

a white purity
of sound
that goes straight
to my heart

right to
where I feel
these things

and I know
that
even though I
am age clumsy

and age foolish

even though I am
age blind
to what surrounds me
in these hasting times

when I hear you
sing
that song that we both
know

I am
a youth

only a youth
again

hide beneath (and burn)

Burning beneath the blue steeples of the larkspur

I
burn lightly
brightly

underneath
the helianthus
I burn
and I hide

and then
the yellow-gold
crinkles into brown

my smoke
becomes
the sky

and the grey descends
to cover me over
as I

burn
beneath

I aspire
and I
desire

open up
my heart
right on my sleeve

where you can
easily
see what I wish

what I
believe

beneath a helianthus
spike
I
I
I

burn higher

I burn again higher

and higher

underneath
the sun

is where I
hide

lucky one

And I long to kneel instantly at your feet

wake
to a shining day

no smoke
no cloud
to play before
my eyes

look across the sky
to the gold
and to the blue

look
all around

earth green and brown

and then I see
a shape I know

busy in the garden

busy
with the singing

busy with
the life that comes
of breathing air
like this

radiating
all
that is good

and I want to throw
myself
down onto my knees
right there
at your feet

these are those days
such
shining days

days
when I know
without a doubt
that
the lucky one
is me

as though (always)

*While all about us peal the loud, sweet Te Deums of the
Canterbury bells*

when the bellringers
for the granite-built cathedral
up on the town's hill
begin their practice

it will be a tuesday evening

always
it is on a tuesday
in the evening

and
I won't notice them
at first

not at all

but they
will know me

yes
they will know me
subconsciously

like a song
seated
back of mind
influencing
without
acknowledgement

so it is
that the music
of the bells
is in me
and I do not know
but
begin to respond

my movements
become
differently fluid

thoughts divert
from where they were
to assume
a kind
of rhythm

reflective
of the clapper sounds
that I cannot yet hear

so that
when my ears
at last
have become attuned
there is no
new knowledge
involved

for I have been
all the while
aware

all the while
un-aware
and yet affected

until my whole being
is encompassed
in the sweet loud sound
of te deums
ringing out
and all around me

and it is
as though
this
has always been

Walk Away Silver Heart – Part 2 (A Muse For The Madonna)

one

sun rises
falls
across your books

physiology
texts
with illustrations

muscle and grist

fascia
and radiating red
depict
the secrets
of a body

I have not
slept well

pace the hallway
the kitchen

subconsciously listening
for a sound of you

who are away
at your studies

walking other paths

beneath
a different sun

two

the breeze
roaming idly
through the oak tree leaves
brings to mind another sound
from a lifetime ago

a voice
never heard before

with an insistent demand
for my attention
to a song
and a singer

the suggestion of a place
to be

an idea
of a someone

me . . .

and a someone . . .

perhaps . . .

me
instantly bereft

in the sure certainty
of non-attraction

lost
before begun

three

the glancing sun
notes the thread
and cloth
of a tapestry

quarter made

abandoned

quarter made
again

a small thing
I do

I know you like it

admire each miniscule
progression
in a persistence
that has carried me
for years

the stitches transform
to your delight
into an image

there comes a point
when I too can see
what it is
that is emerging

but
my pleasure
lies
in the way
that you respond

I stitch
for your joy

for now
though
you are gone
while the cloth
lies still
on the sewing table

and the house
is completely quiet

filled with the hum
of the refrigerator

the birds outside

the traffic
rolling by

there is hardly room
for loneliness
in this intense silence

but
I have become aware
again
of what it is
to be by myself

four

I grind the coffee

you are there
rising up
before me

in the aroma
of this ritual that we live
lies a way
in which
we come alive
within the singing steam
of a percolation
on the stove top

and
in the steam
today
I am seeing you
at work

clay
in your hands

modelling a talisman . . .

    a minor imp

    a devil

    a fallen angel

bake him brown
then
paint him
black

and set him
demon guardian
to watch
the door

five

place your fingers
on the fretboard

place your fingers
to pluck
the strings

let your voice carry
to the garden

I will tend
seedlings
to your song

they grow and flower

seed

self sow

spread
to fill
all the empty spaces

perhaps they move
to the seasons
of your silver tune

I will cut them back
leave
a little room
for other things

you will tell me
what you most desire
to grow

will tell me all
that you wish

six

the next book should be
an anatomy
of the heart

not the muscle

but the emotional
existence
that is
we

and is
us

the next
should be a book
of flame

heat
that will not burn
but
can bring me
to my knees
at your feet

to rest my head
upon you

and
to hold your hand
even now
each time we go out

wherever
we walk

life
is a song
you know

I hear you
singing

life is a song

I know

I know

and this
is the song
of me

seven

and I see you
as though from above

where you go
I must follow

if not by footstep
then
by desire

by wish

by thought and picture
held tight
to me

as though
my sole
remaining passion

and
so it is

for what is there
if there is not
this

what am I
if I am not
of you

this love
is a silvery song

a harmony

I hold the note

I keep the place

I mark the time

sing again

A Kiss For The Worthy

Part 1

This collection is dedicated to the world we live in.

How we are can tolerated,
only heaven knows.

mmm-hmmm (this day)

I CELEBRATE myself, and sing myself

and here I am
the morning come

I rise again
I rise

the sun serves
to illuminate
this world of mine

I rise to kiss
the light

ray
by ray
and beam
by shining beam

I sing
to myself
a satisfaction
for the knowledge
that I *am*

for the *being*
that is me

I laugh
a little dance
as though a stream
a rill
across the smoothing stones
of the woolshed creek

   phwee
   phwee-phwee
   phwee phwee

I whistle to myself
oh
how I love the day

and how
I love
this day

   phwee
   phwee-phwee
   phwee
   phwee

   mmm-hmmm

see then sing (then rise)

And what I assume you shall assume

I
will sing songs
as though
the heavens sang

open up
my voice
with great
conviction

and I
will sing
for you

croon
my love of
being
beneath
a southern sky

let you hear
my heart

its rhythm
beating
beating

beating

and you will see
what I see
through the tenor
of my tones
assume
what I assume
is right
within the song

it is
of a dry
and blue
wide heaven
that I sing

of constellations
that populate the night

the southern cross
and
the pointer

so sing with me

come
sing with me

let us
be
our voices

and rise

note
by note

above ourselves

beyond

in the midst I cannot think

For every atom belonging to me as good belongs to you

it is
difficult

to think

in the presence
of my own
self

there are times
when I . . .

the very *fact*
of me
becomes
overwhelming

it is the awareness
of *being*

the knowledge that
I

    am

my thought
is comprised

compromised

by every atom
belonging to me

establishing *me*
in my own awareness
in such a way that
nothing

no-thing

and
no-*other*-one

is established

what glory
is this

what joy

what knowledge

who
can think
while in the midst

the very midst

of their own
being

is beautiful (this year)

I loafe and invite my soul

I will wander
wool gathering
in my mind

as the wind
blows
stray petals of white blossom
shed by the generosity
of the golden plum
before me

a loaf along

my face
to a breeze
that brings the power
of fragrance

the fresh flowers
of spring

and I
invite my soul
to join me

sing
a sabbatical
pastorale

including
the fleeting flash
of red
and the squeaking pitch
of rosellas
shrilly arguing
in waking branches
of the sentinel oak

what better wool
than this
to gather

what better awareness
of spring

could there be anything
better
than to *be*
residing
as one
with my soul

the pink
of the peach
is beautiful
this year

much like the bees (with your permission)

I lean and loafe at my ease

end of winter

a balmy day

you
sitting in the sun
while I lean

casual

at my ease

watching

bees
are at the blossom
already

the season
will not wait

and your permission
to clear
the garden boxes
becomes a vision
of clarity

to be asserted
where tangles now grow
in obfuscation

I envisage
a time
not long away

of secateurs
and shears
and shovels

happy work
much like the bees
and blooms

but
today
I lean

and contemplate

completely
at my
ease

a kiss (for the worthy)

Observing a spear of summer grass

the susurrations sing
to their gentling
by a breeze

blown a kiss
through
the unbending
spikelets
of chocolate coloured
bulrush flowers

ripened
and waiting to cast seed
into the care
of that fleeting grace

is that not
a tune
worthy of singing

worthy
of a kiss
from zephyr
passing by

atomically speaking

My tongue, every atom of my blood

I speak aloud

speak
with passion
in each utterance

I speak to you

tell you
everything
I
believe in

I talk
to the night as well
and speak aloud
your name

my tongue
finds the way to say

   you

with all of me
entwined
within that word

spoken to you
my words
take
new meanings

with you
listening
what I say
holds
new worth

and I say it
again

say it
aloud

I say it
to you

clean (this soil, my air)

Form'd from this soil, this air

too long
have I
neglected

too few the times
my hand
has reached
to smooth the soil

I know my soul
seeks balm
and know
where
I should seek it

but . . .

so often
my gaze is distorted
through the bending
of a rippled pane

and so often
I wish that I could see
a proof

evidence
of my own making

a boot print
and a thing
of green
and growing

succour for a heart
rising
right from this soil
of mine

breathing my own air

releasing me

to be
again
full cleansed

born here (an immigrant son)

Born here of parents born here from parents the same,
and their parents the same

I come
from a long line
of strangers

born
of here

born
of this

my parents
born
somewhere away
are both
of here
just the same

and theirs before

and theirs
before

came over mountains
crossed
the wilding seas

and they flew
in an airplane

so strange

but
feet on this ground
they were landed
beneath the heavens

      here

into this place
where their lives
new
began

so
sing me a song
of an immigrant
on the road

sing me the song
of a traveller

I will join you
in the chorus
for I carry
that same dusty weight

let us sing
and then be
gone

like the wind
away

I come
from a line
so long of
  strangers
    once

they were strangers
born to be
as one
with *this*
their place

as I
am born to be one
with it

and with this road
that winds

as
it ever
has

soft warnings

I, now thirty-seven years old in perfect health begin

I
once thirty-seven years
and perfect health
was a man

such a man

I was
everything
and every thing
was begun

by me

for me

because
of who and what
I was

I thought myself
so fine

thought myself
so very fine

for I could not conceive
of a thing
that would not
fall
at my feet
when I desired it

thirty-seven
once
I was

everything of me
begun

who could see
and who
could say

that the shimmer
was only
a mirage

a life
equal only
to the swaying
of an illusion

beliefs . . .

a mirage

I look
at thirty-seven
now
and I look beyond
for thirty-six

to whisper
warnings

I whisper
my thirty-six
soft warnings

not until (I die)

Hoping to cease not till death

and
while I breathe
this
clear
honeyed air

while I can taste
the flavours
of a day

this day

my day

I can see I can touch
feel
and hear

I
can inhale

the aroma
that is life

my life

.
.
.

alive

I am alive

and it is so
very good
this ambrosia
of breathing

of being . . .

    me

may I go on
and on

and
may I last

each breath in me

hoping
never to cease

not
until I die

wisdom (but only small)

Creeds and schools in abeyance

and here
I consider for myself
my own inclination
to utterance

what I think

what I
believe

my
leanings

all those things
as yet
by me
unspoken

thoughts
that I choose
not
as yet
to share in words

aloud

they
may bide their time

may wait
for a different
audience

perhaps
I will never let them fly
released
to drift
among the spoken airs

who am I
after all
to speak
my
every passing thought

who am I
to believe
those thoughts
have even
some
small claim

mine is not
a lofty mind

I . . .

am
a poor specimen

raised
from nothing very much
to be . . .

nothing
so very much

and yet

and so

I believe it
wise
with my small allocation
of humility
to keep them

safely

in abeyance

sufficient (at the heart)

*Retiring back a while sufficed at what they are, but
never forgotten*

it is not necess . . .

I mean
don't feel you always mus . . .

come
back here
where I am

it is not
always required
that you take
the lead

sometimes
the mob may run
before you

sometimes
the action seems
up there
way ahead

away ahead

but here is where you are

here
is your
entire world
(this moment)

be at peace
for you suffice
you know

wherever you are
in the teeming
you suffice

and sometimes
you may be unremembered

so it seems
so
it seems

but the heart
of the universe
does not forget
you

always it spins
around
where you stand

so stride
large footsteps
or small

stride out
across the story
of your life

with you
yourself
at the heart
of things

as it should be

you
sufficient
unto yourself

a singing part (of me)

> *I harbor for good or bad, I permit to speak at every hazard*

I watch
a tiny speck
high up in the sky
harassing an eagle

so much ferocity
in one
so small

there is no love
lost
between the hunter
and its prey

but the eagle
is just another bird

its rapt attention
given
to the whole
of each day

there is no good
in it

no bad

and no matter what
may come
the day remains

my love
is for the eagle
for the shape
of it

the grace

and I love
the magpie
for the chortling
of its song

even though
the one
may exact
an existential toll

I keep the song
alive

just as I feel
the day
is alive

I keep it
singing

a part of me

in blossom wild (a nature boy)

Nature without check with original energy

nature boy

creature
of flowers

meadow dancer

yellow
among the daisy
everlastings
and
the growing wild

rumpled
by a breeze unchecked

and blowing . . .

blowing
with all the energy
of a nature boy

forest child

and fauna
that you are

snuffling
and sneezing

the flower
of a blue-gum tree
is the place
you live

a nature boy
in blossom

wild

A Kiss For The Worthy

Part 2

a house filled (with the sensual)

Houses and rooms are full of perfumes

I watch them
in the early morning
hours

they are closed
before the sun

like
little rooms
little houses
un-obtruding
on the lawn

waiting for
daylight proper

and as they open
I realise
they are filled
with sweet perfumes

golden glory

wafted aroma

released now
to attract the buzz
of business

the bees come

they must

and the shape of this
unfolding
day
is revealed

there is pollen
there is
nectar
there is humming
in the air

happy work
and happy
the sensual wafting
of a siren call

the lazy
drift
of sweet perfume

until
the sun wanders
westward

the scent
of ready lust
is withdrawn

little rooms
into
little houses

until tomorrow

gone

what I am (a lapwing's call)

The shelves are crowded with perfumes

I enumerate
the birds
that fill my yard

some days
there is no room
for a man
to walk

for there are ibis
and bower

blackbird

king
and
rosella

silver eye

the wattle-o
with his fire flash
of red
dangled flesh
as an angry declaration
and a look
cast
from a pollen-maddened eye

black and white chortlers
sing
to properly declare
the day

the jackass
laughs
at the evening

and the lapwings
call
a screech of love
in the dead
of night

I take them in

take
all of them
right in

inhale them
as though
they are the scent
that makes me
what I am

every (working) man

I breathe the fragrance myself and know it and like it

and it is
glorious

the sun
warming
across my bent back

and it is
wonderful

the feeling
of this body
working

sweat
on my brow
sweat
rolling down my chest

down my arms

the beauty of a man
at toil

my perspiration
is evaporating
in ripple waves

I breathe
the fragrance of myself
and today
I like it

I am
the working version
of myself
this day

and I am mighty

with bare arms
or spade or axe

I know
this
is a kind
of beauty

I know it is only
because
of what I do

myself

everyman

every working man

I inhale this day
of work
once again
and I like it

I so
do like it

espresso (no and no)

*The distillation would intoxicate me also, but I shall not
let it*

I cannot drink
this beverage
anymore

although
it is right here
by my hand

and right by
the desire
of my heart

I take the beans
that come from
jamaica

beans
that come to me
from india
from senegal
from
I do not know where

but I take them
with their sour smell
of green
and roast them

always turning

always turning them
toward
the brown

heating
until I hear
their song

a percussive tune
of click
on click

of crackling
in the pan

until the sour
is a faded memory
and the aroma
itself
can move the heart

I draw it in

I draw it in

a distillation
that could intoxicate me
were I a weaker being

but
I shall not let it

I know
three cups
is just not right

not right
at all
but
the first cup
is such a pleasure

the second
just happens
somehow . . .

I don't know

a third cup
of this divine transport
would leave me . . .

would take me . . .

I might wake up
still flying
but
more likely
crashed
and burned

I do not care
so much
for rehabilitation

it is a dull
and flavourless
pastime

so
I will be strong
right now
and say no

to my waiting
espresso machine

no
to the beans
I have already ground
(somehow
when I was not attentive)

no
to another
short one
and sharp

no
I will put the coffee
down

here (and there)

The atmosphere is not a perfume

it does not need
to be
a mountain

or the very top
of the tallest
of the poplars
in the township

such locations are
evocative
but the *idea* of them
is enough
to be
my transport

I look to the height
of an oak tree
inhabitant of my back yard
these eighty years

longer
perhaps

the contemplation
is enough

I am there

I am the magpie
perched
on the highest slender branch

swaying

and the atmosphere
I know
is only air
and not perfume
but
it is intoxicating
to me

I close my mouth
and inhale
loud
and deep

it is
the whole earth
that I breathe

risen from the ground

the dirt
the grass

the salt
of a distant sea

I take it in

the top
of my mountain

the tip branch
of my tree

I take it in

I am there
and . . .

and
I
am here

chance encounter (with a lasting liquor)

It has no taste of the distillation, it is odorless

there is
no taste
to this

there is no
odour

there is only
the *I*
of me

the *eau*
of a being

distilled
from what I am
it is
sufficient

the sensation on your lips
is the taste
of a man
alive

and I
bestride
your rapid
thought-ways

I walk
I march
along your covered paths

places
you thought safe
that
you thought
hidden

I will shelter there
for a night
leave my touch
and then
go

for I am the day

I am the night time

I am the light that shines
on you
to confirm
you live

yes
you live

when I am gone
the daze
will be left

the drunkenness
of *is*
the nevermore
of *was*

odourless
and tasteless
it shall be
   you
distilled

remaining
for all time

simply (forever) sensory

It is for my mouth forever, I am in love with it

and I take
the morning

take the rising sun

the new light
and the feeling of dew
still
in the air

I take it in
with my eyes

my ears
hold on to the sounds

and I taste it

this day

another day

who could believe
such luck
and
such wonder

it is in my mouth now
and will be there
forever

oh day

the breath of you
deep
in my lungs

I stand here
and know
what I love

I love
forever

the day (by the bank by the wood) does what it may wish

I will go to the bank by the wood

and is it not
at times
such as these

such trying times as these
that the need
to *be*
emerges

times like these
for *self*
to finally
fully
emerge

on a day of depths
and darkness
before the light
wander
by the embankment

to the secluded place
along the old railway line
in and among
the eucalypts

go there
as you are

your own self

for
who else should you be
on such a day
in such a time
as this

how else can you tell
if this is really
you

strip your clothes
down to the flesh

beyond

strip yourself
until you see
a fleeting glimpse
of what is
your spirit

this . . .

this will be
a day
so like
unlike
any other

and you
will stand still
while it does
what it needs to do

does to you
whatever
it may wish

not much left (of me)

And become undisguised and naked

strip me back
flay
my skin

suspend it
on a low-hung wire

take the meat
away
from the skeleton

weigh
each ingredient
essential

rattle all the bones

there is not much else
that is left
of me

what I
was and
what
I am
and what
I will be

what do you see
when you look
through me

animate my skin
make me dance
all my flesh in a pile
beside me

bones
beating loud
like a drum upon the cavity
of my heart

sending a signal
that

I am
naked

I am undisguised

what you see
are portions
and pieces

traces

of what I was

and that is all
(that is all)
that I
can be

only I

I am mad for it to be in contact with me

heady stuff
the world I breathe

I take in colour
from the leaves

I take in
grey
and white

I absorb the sun

wave
in the breeze

sway

headiness
in contact
with myself

an atmosphere
swooping low
all
around me

I am mad
for it

I am wild
to touch each particle
that motes
the sky

that is *mine*

only *I*
can see it

touch it

only *I*
can breathe it

smell the aroma
of this day

heady stuff

for only
   I

two air (one)

The smoke of my own breath

in the evening
our game
is to intertwine

arms
and legs
as we walk

breath directed
on the diagonal

from my mouth
and lips
to intersect
the soft mist
of breath
from your
mouth and lips

we laugh
at the mingling

your breath
with mine
and mine as one
with yours

we are like two smokers
sharing
what we inhale

after changing it
inside ourselves

to make it your breath
of mist

my breath
of smoke

our air

one

and why

Echoes, ripples, buzz'd whispers

echoes
ripples
those buzzed whispers

caressing
inside my mind

tell me . . .

they are telling me . . .

sometimes . . .

I don't know
what they say

but the message
is an urgency

I feel it
exactly
that way

what will
tomorrow
bring

I wonder
but
I don't know

buzzed whispers
echo

.

.

.

and tell

reveal themselves
in time

show both
answer
and
why

which way (sustained)

Love-root, silk-thread, crotch and vine

I approach
with ultimate
trepidation

ultimate desire

silken threads
run
from me
to . . .

to . . .

what
I wonder

where

down which fork
will I
be drawn

from death
feeling my way
toward
life

toward light

or
do I go
deeper

ever deeper

the love root
is there

bathed
in the light

here
in the darkness
it is only myself

only the *I*
that is changed

which way
do I go

better because

My respiration and inspiration, the beating of my heart

into each
of my contemplations
I place
my heart

the beating
of my heart

to enter thought
requires
the whole of me

or so I believe

so
I believe

with every breath
a new insight

the more I breathe
the more
I know

and so
on twenty-three thousand
occasions
each and every day

I throw myself
the full length
of myself
within

and so
my knowledge grows
and it inspires

twenty-three thousand
times
I find my way
toward light

even now
as I ponder at my ease
this way of thought
is new

and I am more

a bigger
better man
now
because I know

I am more than me
because

I know

the need to test (for life)

The pass-ing of blood and air through my lungs

the feeling of life
that comes
with the first rays
of the sun

when I wake up
to the day

the passing cool of air
filling up my lungs

of blood pumped
around
by my beating heart

I know:

    I am aware

I know:

    I am thinking

and so
I am alive

how could I be
alive
if I did not
really know

sometimes
I need to pinch
myself
to feel the pain

watch
the bloodless whiteness
then
the red

sometimes I speak my
ouch
aloud
just to hear

just
for the sound
of my voice

the little confirmations
and small certainties
available
to be tested

after the night

after
every night

when I
might have died
for all that I know

.

.

.

I wonder
sometimes
how much proof
would prove to be
enough

but
how can I stop

when
is that point
when I no longer need
to know

forgive me
I am tedious
I believe I may have
a small obsession

but the moment
that I stop
is the moment
I no longer know
and truly
I wonder

how
can I be
sure
that I am really
alive

if not
by testing

inhale (my heart)

*The sniff of green leaves and dry leaves, and of the
shore*

I strode the sands
once
of the chelsea
shoreline

walked
through the wavelets
on hampton beach

and where I strode
I raised
the salt flecks
in froth
and in the bubbles

to splash
in the shallows
for me . . .

it was
sublime

but in my heart
I retained
the leaves

the smell of eucalyptus
both dry
and green

I am overwhelmed
by their aroma
when walking
through forest

and I believe
that is where
my heart resides

so I hold
the memories
of salt
inside me

all those times
of white spray
to recall

but I run my feet
through the leaves
at the base
of the woodland

crush
a green leaf

my heart
inhale

a stone (a shell)

And dark-color'd sea-rocks, and of hay in the barn

I keep
on the ledge
in my house
a stone
and a shell

took them
both
from the sea
at lowest water

I left
an exchange

my own footprints
bedded
within the sand

until the tide
swept in
to shore

and I glance
sometimes
at my small
sea stone

dip it
below
an inch of water

to watch the darkness
steal across
yet
make clean

I am a man
of fields
and grasses

my purpose
lies alongside hay
stored
and under cover

my hands
are rough

utility's weapons

and no amount
of water
can make them
gleam

but I recall
a day

one day
of seaside

I recall
the imprint I made
with my naked feet

I left some part
of myself
in that caress
by soft sand

took a stone
and
a shell

for the mark
of me

bad wind (upon your eddies)

*The sound of the belch'd words of my voice loos'd to the
eddies of the wind*

so I stand
to speak

I know that you
can hear me

I know the way my voice
the gout of belching words I utter
and let loose
upon the winds
affects you

fails
to affect you

but

here I stand
and I
will speak

again

I will tell you
of what I know

of what I believe

I will tell
what *is*
the truth of the matter

I will shout
at you
the truth
of the matter

stamp my feet
until I fear
(I hope)
the earth
the very earth
will tremble beneath you

but you

    ha

you
I know
are stoppered

aurally insulated
to filter out
the lesser words

the undesirable

the provocative

and yet
I belch at you
for my world

the world that I
so love

the only world
I can ever know
is burning to ash
in my mouth

released to float
as flecks of grey
blown
in lazy swirling eddies
by your winds

be this (with kisses)

*A few light kisses, a few embraces, a reaching around
of arms*

close your eyes

close them
I say

turn your face
up
to feel the sun
pouring
warm and light
and good
upon it

a benison and boon
that is its own reward
for being

spread wide your arms

feel the breeze
embrace you
surround you
with light kisses placed
as small reminders
of life
that tingle you
at their touch

spread your arms wide

your eyes closed

be them

be this

the benevolence (plays)

*The play of shine and shade on the trees as the supple
boughs wag*

by day I watch
the play of shine
and shade

oak tree twins
that dominate my seasons

how tall is tall

how wide

enough
to be a new atmosphere
when standing
beneath
the leaves

enough to be called home
by the trillers
and warblers
that fill each day

enough
and supple
to reach

to reach toward
the sky

boughs and branches
wag
swaying to a song
sung in gentled whispers
by
the benevolence

the breeze

they are
the instrument
for all the day
to play

baylis street (in a rush)

The delight alone or in the rush of the streets

I wander
streets

as though
I have never wandered
before

these pavements
have the feeling
of *new*
to my feet

treading lightly
with a buoyancy
of delight
that is itself
a rush of sensation

for new streets
are like . . .

in a small way
are like
new planets
where even the atmosphere
must be learned
before the commencement
of true breathing

I could dance
or skip
heels clicking in the air

for the joy
of the new

on these streets I am
in a way
reborn

unseasonably (I wander)

Or along the fields and hill-sides

it is my mind
that does the wandering
not I

I remain
upholstered
in my easy chair

I gaze
unseasonably
at the fire

while my mind
sends reports
in an image stream

a *show*
without
a *tell*

a transportation
enabled
by the dance
of flames

I remember
a murmungee hill-side

a slope
that I perched above

a fog below
that covered
the fields
to make what I saw

a cloud scape

thick enough
that I could
perhaps
step upon it

like a man
crossing water

I feel again
that touch of sun
when I raised my face

closed my eyes

as I close my eyes
now
to feel the fire glow

unseasonably
that kind
of warm

being (the herald)

The feeling of health, the full-noon trill

I rise up

comes the dawn

it heralds me
I
herald the day

and as the grey
retreats
and the green enlivens

the sun shines golden
new light

there is a feeling
of wellness

of health
that is the cycle
of being
once again

and I sing
with a warbling magpie
still learning
the noon day trill

we sing along
with each other

and between us two
the day must know
that it is being

that *we*
are being

and that
heralds the best feeling
that I know

# of day and of rising (to a song)

The song of me rising from bed and meeting the sun

it is a soundless
song

sung by
sensation

sung
by touch

I hear it
before
I open up my eyes

I hear it
through an alteration
in my awareness

I hear it call me
awake

    awake

it is time
to rise

and I find
my feet
have migrated
to the floor
below

suddenly
I am standing

called
to face the window

called to sight the filtered light
streaming in
through veiled curtains

I pull them aside

the song
grows louder now

and inside
I am singing

meet the sun

I
meet the sun

this song
of day

Rescue And Redemption
Part 1

Even in the nether places, love.

Always, love.

blather

S'io credesse che mia risposta fosse

If I but thought that my response were made

how could I explain
the truth

my truth

so at odds
with his

sometimes
I feel that I
have lived
too long

too
over long

and the words that form
inside my mouth
are ancient
understandings

the times
have changed
and he
has no ears to hear
such sentiments

and so
I mumble
crumbs
of now stale
cake

dry

difficult
to swallow

until
one of us
must turn away

heart filled
with
mis-
understandings

and we wonder
each of us
alone

what
just happened

he believed
my answer
was so much cant
and
so much blather

I believed
with all my heart
that I wished
to be heard

by him

this once

this
last time
that I
can love him

yesterday (never does)

here's to you
my darling

here's
to you

ever since you left
I have found myself
secluded

cotton-woolled

alone
in a darkness
of my own making

I could do
this

or
I could do that

I could
so many
many
things

other than hide away
as I do
in the darkness left
behind you

for a time
I hoped
that you would come back
to help me fill the world
around me

for a time
I thought
that yesterday
lived on

it never does
and nor
did you return
into this world
of I
alone

here's to you

here is
to darkness

here
is me

the flickering (stilled)

Questa fiamma staria senza piu scosse

This tongue of flame would cease to flicker

always
the flame has danced

I
have danced along
inside

the flickering
is a sign
of life
a-glow

to dance within
is a sign that reads
alive

that reads
living

it is the soul
I speak of
here

the soul
that is the spark

it is the soul of me
and the way I know
I am one
with all

with
everything

but the flame
is staring
now

the flame
is still

frozen
in mid flicker

no more
tremoring

no more dance

and I
am staring

and still

I
hold no
flicker

and find the flame
gone cold

a sculpture
in colours
correct

the shape
perfect
in contour

but frozen
as my soul
is frozen

empty
of all warmth

I glance around

all else is blue
and white
and shadow

(at least) I will know

Ma percioche giammai di questo fondo

But since, up from these depths, no one has yet

I will say no more
of reasons

madness
is its own
cause

and ever
there is more to find
more
to draw upon

to deploy

and if I did
well
what now
can I tell
to explain it

I grant myself
one respite

only one
that must
suffice

and that is
that I drew away
before completing
execution

each of us
carries
sorry wounds

each of us
not really
healing

each
building moats
and walls
and stately barricades

to weep
behind

and hide
within

to nurse our losses
and begrudgements

my room is small
now

enough
for me

no more
the expansive
the welcoming
the hearty

you must knock
three times

you must rap
a score

you must call my name
aloud
to the heavens
and
at my entryway

I shall not
come

expect no
response

but know that
at some point
I will hear

should you approach
eventually
I
will know

again (a little) again

Non torno vivo alcun, s'i'odo il vero

Returned alive, if what I hear is true

each night
I die
a little

that is the way
the blackness
takes me

un-moving

un-stirring

un-living

only breath
to show I breathe
still

only heart
to know I bleed

I stay the night
not really knowing
there will be
a morning

and
I do not come back
alive
at all

I do not
come back
better

I come back
my mind too full
of all the things I know

of all those things
I know

and I hate the truth
for what it knows of me

I hate the truth
and what it may
reveal

and I hate
the certainty
that I have died
a little
and yet

I will die again
once more

(perhaps) what my belief

Senza tema d'infamia ti rispondo

I answer without fear of being shamed

I only
ever
wished him good

I only wanted
the sweeter things

the better

perhaps though
I came
too close

it may be
that I grew
too large

and possibly
I failed to understand
my own
intentions

but I tell you
as my answer
that I meant him well
and wanted
only
to share
a few steps
upon his way

oh
it may be
in truth
the steps were mine
not his

perhaps
I can admit
that perhaps
I needed
more
than I could say

and
perhaps
I did not know
the power
of my spoken words

perhaps
it was those alone
that smote him

never mind
what I thought
that I
believed

Rescue And Redemption

Part 2

a brief sojourn (in rain)

Let us go then, you and I

would you walk

the day is
un-inviting

sending messages
that tell
of better things
indoors

the rain
is a drizzle
unabated
since the middle . . .

yes
the very middle
of the night

but
if we must
and
if you would
well . . .

a moment

I will retrieve
my hat and coat

my gloves
and boots

so

let us go
then
you and I

shall we sombre
along the path
endeavouring
that our feet
remain dry

or will we
as children
splash and clamber

determinedly
ignoring the sagging damp
that jewels our hats

or shouting
puffs of air
as smoke
that we are breathing

all right
then
I am ready now

let us start
at least
with hand in hand
and well prepared

to catch
one drop each
on outstretched tongues

a laugh
at the beginning
of this
our sojourn

in rain

score (for an evening)

When the evening is spread out against the sky

walk with me

let us stroll
in coats
with deep pockets

so that
when I hold your hand
there will be room
for two

we will push . . .

gently push

a hole
into the gathering grey
until
a moment
when the horizon opens

and the evening
spreads itself
against the sky

the last rays
of sunlight
coloured red

and shaded pink

will linger long
into the twilight

your hand
and mine
will share a pocket

our steps matched
so
for length
of stride

woollen caps
pulled down
over our ears
to keep them warm

my breath
exhaled
and yours
will write the score
of an evening song

to rise
so sung
into the night

in this life (nevermore)

> *Like a patient etherized upon a table*

I roam

my footsteps
stamping
across the world
that is my self

everything
is new

everything about me
pristine

I am not that man

I am not that
was

I am not
the caricature of
me
lying comatose
as though anaesthetized
upon a table

I am
new man

I walk
new walk

I am rediscovered as
quite adequate
to all my own needs

and I can stride
my stage

I can breathe my air

I can sweep the universe
with a glance
and leave it
gleaming

I am not
yesterday

a year ago

the child that was
in a once upon
a long long time
ago

come and take
a new hand
step out into
the new day

take a look
through these
my eyes
at the world transformed

born again

I am quite
born
this time
again

and as the day parts
for me to pass
I know . . .

I know
I will never be
the man
I was

never more
in this life

I
will
be me

a façade (of me and you) on the street

Let us go, through certain half-deserted streets

through
descended darkness

loitering
between streetlamps

the night speaks
step
by step

in echoes
rebounded from the walls
of sundry buildings
wearing
genteel façades

we go
through vacant streets
deserted
with the sun

one fades

the other
disappears

until only we
you
and I
are left
alone together

as we have always been

speaking
to the night
in footsteps
and the tread of shoes

the only voice
a subtle distortion
of ourselves

a façade
of footfalls

an echo

un-alone (au revoir)

The muttering retreats

and so
the day unfolds
inside my head

the voices
at their ease
at last

the muttering
retreats
and I
am left alone

brief moments
falling like a firm blow
of friendly solitude

a sojourn
away
from the perilous

a moment
of
myself

solitaire

and I recall . . .

so briefly
I recall the man I was
when it was only
you and I

I recall
but
truly that is
a *once*

a
was

and now I am
encumbered
by myself

alas
I guess
my moment
is past

the voices surge
once more

so long
old friend

my dearest
dear

until
I surface
from the depths
of me
again

thoughts of you (through cheap red wine)

Of restless nights in one-night cheap hotels

toss
and I turn

awake in the night

I should sleep
I should
close
my eyes

but there is no rest
there is
no
repose

there is only
restless nights
in a one night
hotel

cheap
red wine
into
another darkness
passing
while I think
the same thoughts
over

and over

of you

rescue (and redemption)

And sawdust restaurants with oyster-shells

I am seeking you
within the hubbub
and the burly

trying to gauge
location
by the strength
and timbre
of your voice

rising
and falling
even as you rise
and fall

blows delivered
and blows received

companionable stumbles
to the floor
of this sawdust restaurant
where discarded oyster shell
lies ready
waiting
to slice a knee
or flay a hand

so
where are you
now

high
or low

I stop
to listen

hear
only braying bellows
above the pianola
as I weave
myself
to avoid the worst

it is not
so far a night
of knives
nor yet of guns

mouths and words
fists and knees

boots

there

I hear you again

still shouting
happy

now

now is the time
to seize you
in the grip
of a firm coaxing
of
more pleasure

improved liquor

better company

better fighting

yes
better fighting
at this point in the evening
is an attractive
proposition

for myself

better air
and the chance

the small chance
of a personal
redemption

beyond the blue (a chance)

Streets that follow like a tedious argument

follow me

a moonlit
night

catch a meteor
or
a comet

they fly and fly
the geminids

come
follow me
among them

get on board

and let's explore
beyond
our atmosphere

beyond the tedium
of streetlights

and bitumen
as black
as one
already misplaced
argument

instead
we can look down
on blue

we can marvel
at what
we have left
behind

and remember
what it was
when
it was great

wonderful

come
follow me
beyond our star

let the solar system
languish
while we seek
the new

a place
where we can fall in love
again
with life

re-formed

where tomorrow
is not yet
touched
or spoiled

perhaps
there could be
a chance
beyond this blue
for us to start
again

over again

over

again

words (not today)

Of insidious intent

I cannot write
for you
today

I apologise

I regret

there is no
insidious
intent

no
no

it's just
I cannot place my fingers
on a pen

cannot express
my mood
or feeling

I am
distracted
within myself

and I can find
no word

if I could write
why
I would tell you

of the balm

that comes
with thinking about the words
that I might write
to tell you
of . . .

well . . .

of everything

of anything

of all the things
I think
when I am thinking
about you

my muse of letters

but not
today

I am empty
noting only
a little sunshine

a modest breeze
that ruffles
in a pleasant
passing way

and certain rays
fallen on my face
to warm me

but
not today

I have no
words
for today

by feet (into smoke)

To lead you to an overwhelming question ...

perhaps
a tendril in the air

hovering

smoke
on the breath
of a morning

deep
in the winter
where the white
folds high

as
a snowdrift

an unsullied
sheet

to be written upon

penned
by the feet
of a mouse

leading on
to
a halt

they are
suddenly
gone

maybe
into the air

and you
have been led
by the subtleties
of air
and mouse-pen
to contemplate . . .

an overwhelming
question
lies waiting for you

to unravel
the mist
until
comprehended at last
and released

like smoke

a tendril
in air

the question is

To lead you to an overwhelming question ...

it will take
just
a step

just one small step
and you will be
on the path

with me

we can walk
or run
or
fly a kite

we can
hold
each other's hand

swing along
arm in arm
just
to try it out

a path
sensation

perhaps remarkable

yes
perhaps remarkable enough
to overwhelm
by you
stepping
on to my path

holding my hand

flying
even if
it is just a kite under a sky
that has been painted
a kind of blue

an overwhelming
blue

isn't that
the question

alive (is what you feel)

Oh, do not ask, "What is it?"

I will lead
into
the emotion

let it wash me
until
I feel

until I
am this thing
and
know it

set it free
to know me

I will
transport myself

I will be taken
away

I will
be
as one
saturated top to toe

oh

oh

no no now
do not ask me
what is it

do not say
this
is unwise

step
to me
one heartbeat
at a time

step to me
with faith

believe in me
when I tell you
yes

trust me
to show you
the way

allow the feeling
to take you
wave
by wave

let your emotions
confirm
what is true

close eyes

open
mind

let your imagination
go

let it run wild

laugh
oh laugh

is this not heavenly

laugh
and laugh

this
is being alive

do you not
feel
alive

before the day (becomes old)

Let us go and make our visit

before the day
becomes
too old

before
my mind
finds itself
wandering to other places

and before I decide
a different course
that I might prefer

let us go

let us make
our visit
while a kind thought
still remains

and while
the serenity
of ordered rows
and fresh cut grass
might yet remind

for she loved
the garden

the sun that comes
with spring

and tended
each of her flowers
personally

too sharp
the thorns
yes
but
what is a rose
if not

beauty
has a price
and
she is gone now

so
let us go

while sun
is in the sky

while the clouds
are light
and drifting

we can follow
the breeze
that leads all the way
to that place

only
for one
small
moment

come

before the day
grows
too old

fleet (in corners)

In the room the women come and go

I find myself
a stranger
left
to my own device

inhabiting dim corners
of the room
where women come
and go
to rhythms I have not yet
discerned

my time
is a mystery

and certainties are not
available
to the passing likes
of such
as I

the time it takes
for my instant
to pass
is much the same
as the sway
this way
then that
of a skirt *en-swirl*

and the touch
so fleeting
of florid lips

yet
extended in time
by memory

to endure as
perhaps
a reason
for why I
was

wondrous wondering (and art)

Talking of Michelangelo

maybe
I should seek
my fortune
any other where
than here
but this . . .

this
is the place I know
to be
and to
explore
my most foolish
profound notions

to talk
of this and that

tomorrow
and
tomorrow
still to come

who can tell
where it might
fall

perhaps here
among you
my friends
would be just as well

to speak
of us

of all the moments
that held our
what might be's

as well
I know
to talk of
when we become . . .

all of us

the small da vinci's
of some new art

the paint

the pottery

the lute

the wings . . .

another
cup of coffee here
now
please
for
I must consider
this
some more

let us drink it
black

and let us tell
in wondrous words
of being
michelangelo

stealing (a kiss)

The yellow fog that rubs its back upon the window-
panes

it creeps
it steals
it slithers

covers
like a blanket
fallen

familiar . . .

too
familiar

it reaches
to touch you
close . . .

close
like a lover

rubs its back
against
a window pane

then swirls
into curls
of mesmer

a cold
soft
kiss
and you are breathing it

in

you are breathing it

out

exhale

and it is a risen drift
of grey

into the air

what (feels real)

> *The yellow smoke that rubs its muzzle on the window-*
> *panes*

oh
hush now

the beast remains
without

rubbing a yellow muzzle
on the window pane
it seeks
to capture your attention

to draw your eyes
toward

.

.

.

what

a trail
of something
that was tainted smoke
adrift

up
into the sky

like the flight
of an imagined thought

an imagined
what
might have been

if only . . .

but
it is gone

truly gone

leaving behind it
only the smudge
of a huffed breath

a fog-smear
across the glass
to confirm that something

some thing
truly
was there

it
is gone now

so very gone
yet
the huffing
felt real

we pursue

Licked its tongue into the corners of the evening

shall we pursue
it

this thing
that suggests our names
then runs

leaving a hint

only a small hint
of laughter
in the glee
that lingers in air
we both must pass through

it is a curious thing
and I
do not understand it

nor you

nor you
no

come then
after it

let us track it
and hunt

we can follow the trail
into and out of
places it has tasted
with that suggestive tongue

through every corner
of the evening
come with me

come with me
I feel my appetite
for this
rising

I *hear* it
near now
and singing

a bawdy song
for drinkers

a dancing song
to throw away
false
inhibitions

it makes my feet
skip and jump
and leap
as we pursue

I see you
from the corner of my eye

you
are dancing a little
too

and we run
in time together

footsteps
on the street
as we chase
some elusive elemental

at each corner
I can see
the way it paused
for a while

peered into
the darkness
then shimmied
away
with the night

just out of reach
and just
beyond
my touch

and your touch

but oh
this pursuit is
almost enough

holding hands
and running
with just the vaguest goal
in sight

but perhaps . . .

what if . . .

you
and I
might catch our glimpse

one glimpse
and a thing
to aim for

come run with me
come

let us pursue it

to see

dances (too)

Lingered upon the pools that stand in drains

if I dance
will you
dance

outside
in the darkness
broken by moonlight
filtered
through a drift of clouds

lingering
on the pools of dark water
that dream still dreams
in front of drains
on the street

where I dance

where you dance

come
let us
you and I
just dance

across
and on
within
the lingering light
enticing

that dances
too
upon the dreaming pool

a tortoise (that is new)

Let fall upon its back

before our approaching footsteps
love
like a tortoise
discomposed
has fallen
upon its own back

legs waving
helpless and unknowing
as we approach

each of us
from our own path
and place

neither knowing
until

until

then
at once
it begins its movement

fresh breeze
to
typhoon

and the colours
whirl

and I
do not live
on this planet
any longer

I exist
in some other place

some other
plane

and you are
an *always was*
for me

an *is*

nothing remains
that is not
new

I hold my breath
and spin
around myself

you
stunned soul
the heart of my pivot

an old tortoise
I
wave my arms
my legs

helpless

I
we

approach

existentiality (as startled in the night)

The soot that falls from chimneys

the startle
in the night was
this time
caused by a sound

it woke me

left me wondering
at the source

internal . . .

external . . .

within
or without

it has been a still night
and there is no disguise
available
to deflect
the passing wind
no

a trickle
of sound
as of rain
made fine
but solid
has played patter pit

has woken me

a slight startle
only

but bringing
a sense
an omen of intrusion
from beyond the spaces
that I can control
and manage

inevitably
I examine my heart

seeking
to update its status

whether new harm
has befallen

am I in love
again
or still *in abstentia*

aloof from beauty and wile

from desire
and need

startled
but
as yet
unharmed

no
it beats strongly still

I am reassured
as every *lub*
is followed by its partner
dup

and the situation
is no more
than the soot
that falls from chimneys

is not yet
existential
in its nature

elation (two times)

Slipped by the terrace

these thoughts
run
like water released
at the sharp twist
of a faucet

released
to conceal themselves
as they will
in a game of hide
and find

leap forth
to *surprise*

slip by
on the terrace
where I wander
lost

my own meditations
illuminated
like lightning
strike
in darkness

and I need
to seek
immediately
I need
to seek you out

to tell you
what I
now know

you smile
benevolence
and let me know
that you know
already

and that the thought
has meaning

and that I
have meaning

I am elated
then

now

I am elated
fully

twice

too suddenly

Made a sudden leap

I play
with intuition

tamper
with my future days

I look ahead
I
like to know
what is coming

what
is coming

I make
a sudden leap
because
suddenly
I *do* know

and
I am upon a moment
that is still
to come

I can hold it
in my hands

hold it up
against
the light

keep it
in my pocket
until I'm ready

until
it
is ready

then
I can live it
because
I know it
and it will not hold
a surprise

I do not like
being surprised
by a moment
that leaps up on me
too
suddenly

watching the gold

And seeing that it was a soft October night

while the sun
takes time
to settle

and this
being such a soft night
for october

shall we walk
just
you and I

on the trail
up
to the vineyard

we can watch
to westward
as the changing light
turns the leaves
into
a kind of
gold

just as the grape
becomes
a wine

it will be
a sensual thing

almost
I would like
to touch the leaves

to feel the gold within them

if we go
now
the sun
will take its time
to settle down

we can watch
the gold
become

used to be (then curled up)

Curled once about the house, and fell asleep

the evening news
rises up
to crowd around
the ceiling

think it came
from a fire
many miles away

the world outside
is alight

the bush
is blazing skyward

hearts
are burning
with every leaf
and twig
and branch
that dances flame

and it is all across
the nightly reportage

the reds
and yellows
violently seeking an escape
from behind the flat screen
where they
temporarily
dwell

the smoke
at bulletin end
curled around the room

curled round
and around
descending at last
to sleep
in a corner

I
do not sleep

I
cannot sleep

I see and feel
the visions
of what used
to be

as much as is needed

And indeed there will be time

though the light
is more
of evening
than the harsher hues
of midday
still
it remains

still
I can see

and though
the darkness
is less
a stranger
than once it was
well . . .

that is nothing

not really

there will be time
left
for you and I
to speak

time left to share
a body-shake
of laughter
even though
we end up in tears

holding each other

weeping
just a little
for what has been

but still
we both know
there is a lifetime
in a look

eternity
in silence
that lasts just as long
as we need

we've said it all
many times
and there is no joy
in being mundane
now

there will be time
for that
no shortage

after

we did some things
you and I
we did
do those things
didn't we

I would not want
to do them
again

but
there is pleasure
in having time left
to remember

do you recall . . .

I know
that you do

and you

you

know
now
that I do
too

back (into grey)

For the yellow smoke that slides along the street

the fog rolls in
through the streets
of my town

the shade
shifts
from black night
into grey

and my feet
sound

clear
beneath the shroud

.

.

.

closer
to a streetlight
colour
lives

suddenly
it is yellow smoke
that slides

into
a bus shelter

across
the slatted rest
of a curb-side seat

dancing
in the damp
fogged motes
of warm light

until I fade
clarity
by clarity

pace by pace

back into a grey shade
then
to night

well done (the day)

Rubbing its back upon the window-panes

it is a day
filled with light
from
first dawn

all through its hours
no cloud
no doubt

and in the afternoon
coming on
to evening

it rubs its back
job done
against a window pane

I have been riveted
just watching

being

as another day
unfolded

little tears
and little dramas

minute triumphs
and small pains

the day
is done
and the job
is done

all
is done
quite well

for everything

There will be time, there will be time

wait

the season
will change

see
even now
the tree
is emerging

flowers come

as clouds
drift by

your last thought
is gone
succeeded
by the coming one

a day starts

another
ends

whatever
is to be next

there will be
time

there will
be time

for being
you
for being new
for being
too
for you
and me
enough to see
time
to feel . . .

free

time
time
time
time

there will be

time
time
time
time

enough

white face (and rhyme)

To prepare a face to meet the faces that you meet

mirror you
and mirror
me

take the paste
and slather

make a moue
amid
the lather

smooth it down
pat-a-cake
slap it slip
into
a face-like shape

mould your visage
as I do
mine

meet my true face
first grin
in line

then
turn around
your courage built
to meet
the faces rushing

rushing

on
the street

hold your head
up
you are not alone

I'll hold
my head up
two
as one

and step in time
your step
with mine

we mime we mime
two clowns
silently
in rhyme

novel advice (my darlings)

There will be time to murder and create

always kill
your darlings

sage advice
for one and all

you need
to kill your darlings
but . . .

all in time

you can take it
slow

first
build them up
with
all your heart

make them ring clearly
sound
and true

make them
loveable

likeable
and hateful
both

essential

critical

unimaginable

make of them
the pumping heart

that reveals the story
with each beat

take your time
write
what you want
and then . . .

and then . . .

commit a little mayhem

don't hesitate
to dramatize

let chaos rule
throughout
the world

always
the way you guide

and no need to explain
your why
to anyone

why did you
kill
our darlings

why not keep them

were they not
good

*we all feel
so
vulnerable
with our darlings
gone*

and wonder

we wonder

*what will happen
to us
in the chapter
that you write
next*

time and hands (in the river)

And time for all the works and days of hands

say
to the river
there is time

say to the breezes
there is time

say it to the sky
shout it
toward heaven

for all
who can hear
there is time

time
to remember
all the wrongs
(yea
all the rights)

time to take
a moment
of reflection

time enough
for everything

for the work of these
my hands

there is time

if there is daylight
there is time

don't I know
the hourglass
is pouring sand
(my sand
yes
I do)

don't I know
each moment
is a pearl
(I know
I know
it is true)

don't you think I know
the hour
is coming
(here it is
oh
here
it is)

I know
but
for me
there still seems
time

time is a circle
I
am rounding

time
is ninety degrees
in the corner
of a square

I will come
to where I started
I will be
the way
that I was
then

and the time
for these hands
to be working
will be done

holding on (to questions)

That lift and drop a question on your plate

and
are we not
at the end
of times

you and I

we spend hours
in contemplation

self

other

out there

within

and all the ways
of thought
and wonder
lead
toward conclusion

the search for answers
results
in questions
dropped squalling
as though from the wide blue

as though
from the heart
of storm

from nether regions
not visited
but dreamt

the end of times
my apocalypse-o

we should pack
all our bags
and baggage

but
I look at you
and wonder
again

where

where for you

where
for me

.
.
.

take my hand

forget all that
and take my hand

until the end

let us
hold

ocean (time)

it is
a river

running from somewhere
that was
the start

it is a flow
that washes
by the place
my feet have found

it is a silver line
leading
into the distance
until it fades

and somewhere
far enough
ahead
that I cannot see

it is the ocean

waiting patient
until I become
as one
with the waving
of a tide
that ebbs
and flows

yet
there is time
enough
for all that I must do

and
there is time enough
I think
for you to do what you must do
as well

time enough
to join the river
and to twirl
a while
in idled eddies
on the way

until the sea of time
brings us
to ocean side

that great repository
of everything
that is that was
that
could have been

one day

soon enough

no hurry

time

# of rock pools (and responses)

And time yet for a hundred indecisions

it is the case
that . . .

oh
I don't know

I find myself
in situations

and the splash
of softened water
in the confines
of the pool
brings me
acutely
to the knowledge
of another

I realise
again
that there are points
beyond returning

and a question hovers
just there
beyond my reach

do I allow
the hand that
even now
is seeking purchase
in the vicinity
of my knee

prelude to love
perhaps
down
among the suds

to the quiet
rhythmic pulse
of an electric motor

making bubbles
swirl
while concealing traces
minimal

suggestions
that are a naked body
at full languish

time

time

to rise
or to recede

as the tide
alternately exposes
and then subsumes
the eager pools
carved
spa-like
along a rocky shore

eagerness
yes

eagerness yes yes
but . . .

oh
a first touch
that is a fingertip
that is
a shiver

exploring
through the froth

seeking
an urgency
in the answer
to a question

you and me (at three o'clock)

three o'clock
is a patter
of rain
and memories

moving pictures
in the theatre
of the mind

sometimes
it seems the past
is a treasure house
of moments lost

of choices taken
now subject
to revision

it has been
a long journey
this

filled
with instances of you
and me

the you
has sometimes
come and gone

different faces
temporarily in situ

the me
always the same

no matter how
different
always the same

trying hard

eternally striving

reaching with such
intense
endeavour

while erring
in recurrent patterns

minutely changed
with each new occasion
of you

your every
incarnation

at three o'clock
sometimes
a different
same old
situation
comes alive
again

playing
in the theatre
that reels inside
my head

and I know
the ways
I could have changed
the outcomes

but

tcha

tcha

what point
when
here we are

this moment
now
this
you
and this me

while three o'clock
is only ancient visions
played
with an impoverished
recall

out
my light

out
right now

I wish
to sleep

a breakfast taken (deshabille)

Before the taking of a toast and tea

it becomes
a breakfast
taken in your bed

a straightening
of sheets
before the toast

two pieces
for me

and nothing said
of
the deshabille
that decorates
the corners

memories
of the night
that is now
gone

coffee
to damp down
stale breath

a question
suspended
in the air

a glance across
to determine
if
all is well
in aftermath

a half-embarrassed
chuckle
emerges reluctantly
at a vivid memory
flashing past

another glance

another question

tentative
a hand
and
an unexpected
electricity

the toast
is crumbs
abandoned

the coffee
cold
a brown mark left
upon the cup

becomes
a breakfast

taken
in your bed

the dregs say (it is time)

In the room the women come and go

the courtesan
today
has put her time
in

coffee now

a short black
is all the time left
on this roster

a finger
touches make-up
but
not important
anymore

there is no longer thought
of customers
come and gone
and
come
and gone again

a little drop
of something
to flavour
the caffeine

a chat
about a child
and school
and mortgages
with a colleague

street clothes
in the lounge
while negligees
drift by

leading charcoal suits
that come
before they go

read the dregs
left to run
down the sides
of an upturned cup

search
for coffee words
and symbols
meaning . . .

nothing there
but broken paths
uncertain runs
and rivulets

little signs that say

*it's time
to go home*

more (the same) like you

Talking of Michelangelo

what I am
from
what I've been

every breath
taken in
has changed me

words
that I have spoken

and
tears I shed
in anguish

what is
I
is now
not
what *I* once was

a sculpture
that
reshapes
at every blinking
of an eye

and I shape
myself
a little more
like you

as we walk out
together
the length
of my step
is changed

the thoughts
that I allow
to represent me

the stature
I assign
to who
I believe I am

a little more
like you

a little more
the same

The Original Project Responses

My initial responses and submissions (written for the original collaborative
project around 2001) were the following poems:

For Amy Lowell's *Madonna Of The Evening Flowers* the poems *the sun
shines in on your books* and *cool, like silver.*

For Walt Whitman's *Leaves of Grass*, the poem *the atmosphere is not a
perfume.*

Finally, for T.S. Eliot's *The Love Song of J. Alfred Prufrock*, the poem *no not
the old city*.

These responses to those marvellous original poems are included below,
and it will be evident to any reader that they were written at a very
different stage in this poets development, compared to the newer work
above.

the sun shines in on your books

The sun shines in on your books

I immerse myself in your pictures,
sketched in the clarity of cold
night without moon. Sharpness of
line and image.
You draw me in, watching
the pale detail of a white lily emerge
beneath your hand. Erupted
yellow, the core.

I am walking in your world,
a journeyman of word reflections
from the mirror pools of observation
and chance encounter,
marked by typeface on white paper.
Mood and manner, mind and heart.
Extracts from the seizure of a moment
frozen in time.

I watch you move around your drawings,
from the near side of the bed,
as the sun streams in on your books,
on your folio,
and on your body bent to raise
the lily in the slow light of morning.
I picture you in words.

cool like silver

You are cool, like silver

Cool, she was, like silver. Dapples
on the rolling, falling waters
of a stream come out of sunrise,
sliding to glisten. On the rocks
as smooth as thigh out-stretched,
she taught the way. To reach
and to become as one
with flowing water, to know its secrets
and the treasure of eddied places,
to slow measure a path across the bed,
through rapids and turbulence. Don't
rush, don't fall.

Cool she was, like silver trapped
or caught. Inside a playground of
the moon, under a soft light and
shining. A waving dance
of shimmers, to mesmerise. Me?
I was lost. In time, control,
and knowledge far too early. For
the coolness of her silver
purchased only one long shiver. I
could not heed, nor halt. So fast,
too fast expired, I could not slow and
I, could not go on.

the atmosphere is not a perfume

The atmosphere is not a perfume

this atmosphere is not a perfume
but is the presence that still remains
in contours shaped when you rose to leave
with morning

I am embracing the slow escape of warmth
to find comfort in this chilling room
making your image in
the smoke of my own breath
and half day-dreaming

what I cannot do is hold you
grasp as I might to catch the illusion
there is nothing but the trace
left in a tepid fold of cloth
that holds a whisper of the smell of you
and it is my skin that lies alone
bare against the sheets
and last desire

no not the old city

Streets that follow like a tedious argument

and the old city is a wasting of time   there is
nothing of value there
no return on that investment   those twenty years
of purgatude
spent with an aspirational heart   every day
from the beginning
when to walk that way was something fresh and
new   each pace
holding its own speed and reason   much like
here   perhaps
here   in this newer place   with this newer
purpose
so draped with the coatings   now   of
experience   knowledge
perhaps it is not the purpose that has changed
not so very much

this though   this is not that ancient wreckage
with its labyrinth byways
foetid distractions   those twisted streets that
follow like a tedious argument
renewed afresh upon boulevards and avenues that
open   yawning black
in sickly   honeyed   invitation with each tempted
visitation to that past   no
this is newer ground   these paths are fresh and
open   look up
that blue is the sky   in this place it is mine
yours   ours   if you wish it
you and me   and the coloured blue of our own
sky

no   let us not go near to the old city
there is nothing there for us   nothing

Source Materials

Madonna of the Evening Flowers - Amy Lowell

In *Walk Away Silver Heart*, I have worked with the Lowell poem, *Madonna of the Evening Flowers* . In my reading, this was a love poem, written as a personal one-to-one communication from the heart.

The poem had two distinct moods, reflecting initial absence of the beloved one, and then the Madonna in her element.

A lovely poem to read and contemplate.

Madonna of the Evening Flowers

All day long I have been working
Now I am tired.
I call: "Where are you?"
But there is only the oak tree rustling in the wind.
The house is very quiet,
The sun shines in on your books,
On your scissors and thimble just put down,
But you are not there.
Suddenly I am lonely:
Where are you?
I go about searching.

Then I see you,
Standing under a spire of pale blue larkspur,
With a basket of roses on your arm.
You are cool, like silver,
And you smile.
I think the Canterbury bells are playing little tunes,
You tell me that the peonies need spraying,
That the columbines have overrun all bounds,
That the pyrus japonica should be cut back and
rounded.
You tell me these things.
But I look at you, heart of silver,
White heart-flame of polished silver,
Burning beneath the blue steeples of the larkspur,
And I long to kneel instantly at your feet,
While all about us peal the loud, sweet Te Deums
of the Canterbury bells.

Amy Lowell - 1919

Leaves of Grass - Walt Whitman

A Kiss For The Worthy has worked with the Whitman poem
Leaves Of Grass.

This is a vast piece of poetry that Whitman spent much of his lifetime
revising and rewriting and republishing. The relevant extract follows.

Song of Myself (Leaves of Grass)

1

I CELEBRATE myself, and sing myself,
And what I assume you shall assume,
For every atom belonging to me as good belongs
to you.

I loafe and invite my soul,
I lean and loafe at my ease observing a spear of
summer grass.

My tongue, every atom of my blood, form'd from
this soil, this air,
Born here of parents born here from parents the
same, and their parents the same,
I, now thirty-seven years old in perfect health
begin,
Hoping to cease not till death.

Creeds and schools in abeyance,
Retiring back a while sufficed at what they are, but
never forgotten,
I harbor for good or bad, I permit to speak at
every hazard,
Nature without check with original energy.

2

Houses and rooms are full of perfumes, the
shelves are crowded with perfumes,
I breathe the fragrance myself and know it and like
it,
The distillation would intoxicate me also, but I
shall not let it.

The atmosphere is not a perfume, it has no taste
of the distillation, it is odorless,
It is for my mouth forever, I am in love with it,
I will go to the bank by the wood and become
undisguised and naked,
I am mad for it to be in contact with me.

The smoke of my own breath,
Echoes, ripples, buzz'd whispers, love-root, silk-
thread, crotch and vine,
My respiration and inspiration, the beating of my
heart, the pass-ing of blood and air through my
lungs,
The sniff of green leaves and dry leaves, and of
the shore and dark-color'd sea-rocks, and of hay in
the barn,
The sound of the belch'd words of my voice loos'd
to the eddies of the wind,
A few light kisses, a few embraces, a reaching
around of arms,
The play of shine and shade on the trees as the
supple boughs wag,
The delight alone or in the rush of the streets, or
along the fields and hill-sides,
The feeling of health, the full-noon trill, the song of
me rising from bed and meeting the sun.

Walt Whitman - 1855

The Love Song of J. Alfred Prufrock - T. S. Eliot

Rescue and Redemption derived from my reading of Eliot's *Prufrock* as a journey in search of love. Perhaps with a companion, or *for* a companion. Often into the less salubrious places.

It is a poem of massive scope, with the epigraph at the beginning serving, for me, the role of *Requiem*. The relevant sections of the poem follow.

The Love Song of J. Alfred Prufrock

S'io credesse che mia risposta fosse
A persona che mai tornasse al mondo,
Questa fiamma staria senza piu scosse.
Ma percioche giammai di questo fondo
Non torno vivo alcun, s'i'odo il vero,
Senza tema d'infamia ti rispondo.

Let us go then, you and I,
When the evening is spread out against the sky
Like a patient etherized upon a table;
Let us go, through certain half-deserted streets,
The muttering retreats
Of restless nights in one-night cheap hotels
And sawdust restaurants with oyster-shells:
Streets that follow like a tedious argument
Of insidious intent
To Lead you to an overwhelming question ...
Oh, do not ask, "What is it?"
Let us go and make our visit.

In the room the women come and go
Talking of Michelangelo.

The yellow fog that rubs its back upon the window-
panes,
The yellow smoke that rubs its muzzle on the
window-panes,
Licked its tongue into the corners of the evening,
Lingered upon the pools that stand in drains,
Let fall upon its back the soot that falls from
chimneys,
Slipped by the terrace, made a sudden leap,
And seeing that it was a soft October night,
Curled once about the house, and fell asleep.

And indeed there will be time
For the yellow smoke that slides along the street,
Rubbing its back upon the window-panes;
There will be time, there will be time
To prepare a face to meet the faces that you meet;
There will be time to murder and create,
And time for all the works and days of hands
That lift and drop a question on your plate;
Time for you and time for me,
And time yet for a hundred indecisions,
And for a hundred visions and revisions,
Before the taking of a toast and tea.

In the room the women come and go
Talking of Michelangelo.

T. S. Eliot - 1915

More Informtion

Basic information on the lives of Amy Lowell, Walt Whitman and T.S. Eliot have been sourced from Wikipedia.

I have accessed the source poems for this project from the following online locations:

The Reader (Lowell)
The Walt Whitman Archive (Whitman)
The Poetry Foundation (T. S. Eliot

I commend these wonderful organisations, and wonderful poets to you.

FP

Index of Individual Poems

A

B

C

Author Information

About the Author

Frank Prem has been a storytelling poet since his teenage years. He has been a psychiatric nurse through all of his professional career, which now exceeds forty years.

He has been published in magazines, online zines, and anthologies in Australia, and in a number of other countries, and has both performed and recorded his work as spoken word.

He lives with his wife in the beautiful township of Beechworth in North East Victoria, Australia.

Connect with Frank

As the author, I hope you enjoyed this volume of poetry collection. I think that mine is a unique style of writing that can appeal well beyond a *'pure poetry'* readership.

If you enjoyed it, I'd like to ask you to do two small things for me.

First leave a short comment about the book with your preferred online retailer by leaving a customer review.

Online reviews provide social proof to readers and are critical to Indie authors such as myself.

The second thing is, please pop over to my author page **www.FrankPrem.com**, and subscribe to receive my occasional Newsletter.

From time to time I'll let you know what is happening with myself and my writing, as well as keeping you informed of any giveaways I may be planning.

You can also find me on **Facebook**, **Twitter**, **Instagram** and **YouTube**.

Other Published Works

Free Verse Poetry

Small Town Kid (2018)

Devi l In The Wind (2019)
 s
The New Asylum (2019)

Herja, Devastation - With Cage Dunn (2019)

Walk Away Silver Heart (2020)

A Kiss for the Worthy (2020)

Rescue and Redemption (2020)

Pebbles to Poems (2020)

The Garden Black (2022)

A Specialist at The Recycled Heart (2022)

From Volyn to Kherson (2023)

Ida: Searching for the Jazz Baby (2023)

Picture Poetry/Spoken Image

Voices (In The Trash) (2020)

The Beechworth Bakery Bears (2021)

Sheep On The Somme (2021)

Waiting For Frank-Bear (2021)

A Lake Sambell Walk (2021)

What Readers Say

Small Town Kid

A modern-day minstrel. Small-Town Kid is a wonderful collection

—S. T. (Australia)

A poet's walk through his childhood in a small Australian town.

—J. L. (USA)

Devil In The Wind

Instantly grips you by the throat in his step-by-step story of survival. Bravo!

—K. K. (USA)

Outstanding!

—B. T. (Australia)

The New Asylum

Words can't do justice to the emotional journey I travelled in (reading this collection).

__C. D. (Australia)

If I had to pick one book over the past year that has truly resonated with me, this would be it.

__K. B. (USA)

Sheep On The Somme

Museums and archivists take note--sell this in your gift shops, preserve it in your archives. Professors, teachers--share with your students.

—A R C (United States)
 (This) book is a beautiful and graphic tribute to all those brave men and women who gave their lives for their countries between 1914 and 1918.

—R C (South Africa)

Ida: Searching for The Jazz Baby

I found myself deeply moved by the presentation of Ida's elusive, illusionary life.

—E G (United States)

He gives her a depth and vulnerability that the press didn't.

— A C (United Kingdom

The Garden Black

Prem creates verse that illuminates our world, its experiences and history.

—S C (United Kingdom)

Prem's poetry reminds that life is fragile and fleeting ... both harsh and beautiful.

—D G K (United States)

Simply written, powerfully felt.

__C. (Australia)

As a combination of poetry, prose, and wonderfully ominous illustrations, I found Herja, Devastation refreshingly original.
 Highly recommended!
—G. B. (AuBravo!

—K. K. (USA)

Outstanding!

—B. T. (Australia)

www.FrankPrem.com